F Horn

Easy Great Carols

Instrumental Solos for the Intermediate Soloist

Contents

TRACK		PAGE
1	TUNING NOTE A CONCERT	
2	TUNING NOTE B♭ CONCERT	
3/13	HARK! THE HERALD ANGELS SING	4
4/14	SILENT NIGHT	6
5/15	WE THREE KINGS	8
6/16	GOD REST YE MERRY, GENTLEMEN	10
7/17	JOLLY OLD ST. NICHOLAS	11
8/18	PAT-A-PAN	12
9/19	AWAY IN A MANGER	13
10/20	UP ON THE HOUSETOP	14
11/21	WE WISH YOU A MERRY CHRISTMAS	16
12/22	COVENTRY CAROL	18

CURNOW MUSIC

Selected by James Curnow

Easy Great Carols
F / E♭ Horn

Arranged by:
Stephen Bulla
Douglas Court
James Curnow
Paul Curnow
Timothy Johnson

Order number: CMP 0924.04
ISBN 90-431-2031-6
CD number: 19.052-3 CMP

Easy Great Carols

INTRODUCTION

These carols, collected from around the world, include both sacred and whimsical selections. The arrangements have been created by some of the foremost writers of instrumental music, who are internationally known for their musical compositions and arrangements. The goal of these arrangements is to allow the instrumentalist the opportunity to give praise and adoration to God through their musical abilities.

There is a separate piano accompaniment book available. This accompaniment book will work with all of the soloist books. When an accompanist is not available, the accompaniment CD (included) can be used for performance. This CD will also allow the soloist to rehearse on their own when an accompanist is not available.

The accompaniment CD contains tuning notes at the beginning to allow the soloist to adjust their intonation to the intonation of the compact disc accompaniment. Each arrangement in this collection includes a sample performance with soloist as well as a track with just the accompaniment.

May you enjoy using this collection and find it useful in extending your musical ministry.

Kindest regards,

James Curnow
President
Curnow Music Press

1. HARK! THE HERALD ANGELS SING

Track: 3 13

Arr. **James Curnow** (ASCAP)

2. SILENT NIGHT

Arr. **Paul Curnow** (ASCAP)

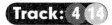

3. WE THREE KINGS

Arr. Timothy Johnson (ASCAP)

Track: 5 15

Tranquilly (♩ = 90)

4. GOD REST YE MERRY, GENTLEMEN

Arr. **Stephen Bulla** (ASCAP)

Moderately fast (♩ = 84)

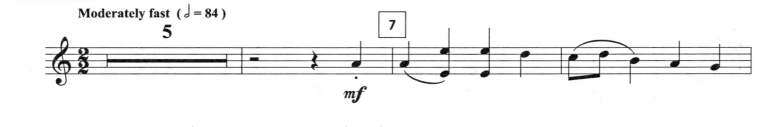

5. JOLLY OLD ST. NICHOLAS

Track: **7** 17

Arr. **Douglas Court** (ASCAP)

Fast and lively
(♩ = 116)

6. PAT-A-PAN

Arr. **Stephen Bulla** (ASCAP)

Track: 8 18

7. AWAY IN A MANGER

Arr. **James Curnow** (ASCAP)

Moderately slow, with expression (♩ = 76)

(Traditional American Tune)

(Traditional English Tune)

CMP 0924.04 F / E♭ Horn

Copyright © 2004 by **Curnow Music Press, Inc.**

13

8. UP ON THE HOUSETOP

Theme and Mini Variations

Arr. **Paul Curnow** (ASCAP)

9. WE WISH YOU A MERRY CHRISTMAS

Track: 11 21

Arr. **Douglas Court** (ASCAP)

16

10. COVENTRY CAROL

Arr. **Timothy Johnson** (ASCAP)

Track: 12 22

TONS OF TUNES for Church   Grade 0.5-1
• arranged by Mike Hannickel and Amy Adam

A collection of 32 'fun to play' melodies arranged in easy keys for
beginner instrumentalists. All the Tons of Tunes for Church books can be
used together to form an ensemble. Chord symbols are included in the
Piano Accompaniment book for keyboard or guitar. Titles include, Abide
With Me, Now thank We All Our God, Swing Low Sweet Chariot,
Onward Christian Soldiers and many more. A separate piano
accompaniment book is available for concert performances.
Order number: 0873.03 CMP

          0869.03 CMP Piano Accompaniment

TONS OF TUNES for the Beginner   Grade 0.5-1
• arranged by Mike Hannickel and Amy Adam

Fun and familiar tunes that beginners love to play!
There are two things that beginners really want to do: 1) play songs they
RECOGNIZE and 2) play the TUNE. In TONS OF TUNES for the
BEGINNER many of the easiest of familiar songs are gathered together
so that young musicians can do just that - play the tunes to familiar
music! Most of the songs can be performed by players who have learned
only a few notes. Play along with the CD accompaniment or with any
combination of solo instruments for tons of practice fun!
Order number: 0669.02 CMP

          0672.02 CMP Piano Accompaniment

TONS OF TUNES for the Holidays   Grade 0.5-1
• arranged by Mike Hannickel and Amy Adam

This collection of the easiest holiday melodies allows your beginning
students to have fun playing their favorite seasonal music! Any
combination of solo instruments can play together. Organized by order
of difficulty, these familiar songs and the included accompaniment CD
are sure to motivate your students. Practice and perform with the CD
accompaniment or buy the separately available piano part. Your students
will want to use TONS OF TUNES for the HOLIDAYS year after year!
Order number: 0695.02 CMP

          0699.02 CMP Piano Accompaniment

Eb Horn

EasyGreat *Carols*

Instrumental Solos for the Intermediate Soloist

Contents

TRACK		PAGE
1	TUNING NOTE A CONCERT	
2	TUNING NOTE Bb CONCERT	
3/13	HARK! THE HERALD ANGELS SING	22
4/14	SILENT NIGHT	24
5/15	WE THREE KINGS	26
6/16	GOD REST YE MERRY, GENTLEMEN	28
7/17	JOLLY OLD ST. NICHOLAS	29
8/18	PAT-A-PAN	30
9/19	AWAY IN A MANGER	31
10/20	UP ON THE HOUSETOP	32
11/21	WE WISH YOU A MERRY CHRISTMAS	34
12/22	COVENTRY CAROL	36

Curnow MUSIC

Selected by James Curnow

1. HARK! THE HERALD ANGELS SING

Arr. **James Curnow** (ASCAP)

Copyright © 2004 by **Curnow Music Press, Inc.**

2. SILENT NIGHT

Arr. **Paul Curnow** (ASCAP)

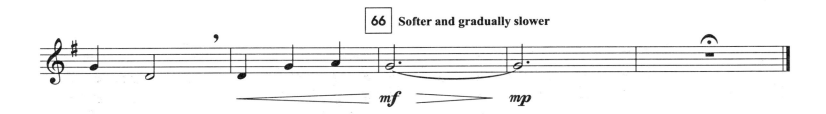

3. WE THREE KINGS

Arr. **Timothy Johnson** (ASCAP)

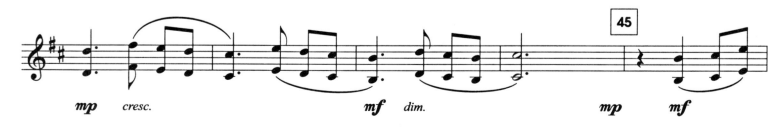

4. GOD REST YE MERRY, GENTLEMEN

Track: 6 16

Arr. **Stephen Bulla** (ASCAP)

5. JOLLY OLD ST. NICHOLAS

Arr. **Douglas Court** (ASCAP)

CMP 0924.04 F / E♭ Horn

6. PAT-A-PAN

Arr. **Stephen Bulla** (ASCAP)

7. AWAY IN A MANGER

Arr. **James Curnow** (ASCAP)

8. UP ON THE HOUSETOP
Theme and Mini Variations

Arr. **Paul Curnow** (ASCAP)

9. WE WISH YOU A MERRY CHRISTMAS

Track: 1121

Arr. **Douglas Court** (ASCAP)

10. COVENTRY CAROL

Arr. **Timothy Johnson** (ASCAP)